FUN PHONICS MANIPULATIVES

Quick and Easy Flip-Books, Pull-Throughs, and
Interactive Mini-Books to Make and Share

··

by Michelle Hancock,
Sheryl Pate, and
Jennie VanHaelst

SCHOLASTIC
PROFESSIONAL BOOKS

New York • Toronto • London • Auckland • Sydney

Dedication

To our families and friends who gave us support and
encouragement while working on the book. We wish to thank
the students and parents for their feedback on the materials.
A special thanks to Terry Cooper and Ingrid Blinken from
Scholastic for their advice and support on the project.

Cover and interior design by Sydney Wright
Cover and interior illustrations by Rusty Fletcher

ISBN: 0-590-31469-6
Printed in the U.S.A.

Contents

Introduction

Welcome to *Fun Phonics Manipulatives* a collection of multi-sensory, hands-on materials we created to help students learn letter/sound correspondences and develop a strong sight word vocabulary. Phonetic pull-throughs, predictable books, and flip-books invite children of various learning styles and strengths to build and play with rhyming words in a fun way. Recognizable pictures provide visual hooks, giving children an association for remembering letters and sounds. As children use these materials, we find that they picture the easily identifiable illustrations for the rhyming words in their minds when they encounter new words with the same blends. Whether for initial consonants or for rhyming word blends, these picture associations help children make that critical link between meaning and memory.

Whatever your approach to teaching reading, you'll find that these pull-throughs, predictable books, and flip-books can enrich your program. If your classroom reading program is phonics- or skill-based, these materials will fit right in. In a whole language-based program, the materials provide a natural extension for use with other literature. Here's how phonetic pull-throughs, predictable books, and flip-books work. (More detailed descriptions, directions, and extension activities are included with each set of patterns.)

Phonetic Pull-Throughs:

These appealing manipulatives use visual clues to help children make letter/sound associations. Each pull-through is shaped to represent one of the rhyming words in a group. For example, children make a dog-shaped pull-through for rhyming words with the *og* blend, starting with the word *dog*. As children begin to associate the rhyming blend with the picture, they can make the letter/sound link with words in other contexts.

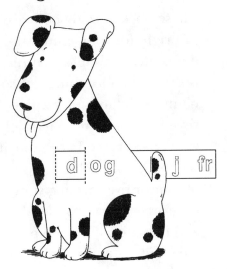

Pull-Through Predictable Books:

Children add as many pages as they wish to these books, with covers that feature pull-through initial consonant strips. On each new page they add, children fill in a blank to complete a sentence such as "*I wear a _____ hat.*", creating a predictable book they can read. You can use pull-through predictable books to focus on initial consonants, to teach vowels, or to support a class theme.

Flip-Books:

These pocket-sized books are just right for your young students. Recognizable pictures provide clues for initial consonants as children play with rhyming words and build sight word vocabulary. Each self-correcting book teaches a group of four or five rhyming words—reinforcing rhyming blends and helping children experience success in remembering letter/sound associations.

Introducing Phonetic Pull-Throughs, Predictable Books, and Flip-Books:

We like to pick and choose from the three manipulatives depending on our particular grade level, the themes or letters we are focusing on, and our students' interest. We've organized each section of this book alphabetically by vowel because that is the way our language arts curriculum is designed. We've also found that it is easier for our students to grasp the letter and the sound *Aa* than it is for them to grasp the letter and the sound *Uu*. However, you can use the materials and patterns in this book in any order you choose, in whatever way they best support your program.

We've found that it works well to introduce pull-throughs, predictable books, and flip-books in small group settings, guiding students in making and reading the materials the first time through. With our kindergartners, we usually introduce the first pull-through at the beginning of the second

month of school and add a new pull-through every two weeks. As the children learn concepts about print and become familiar with predictable books, by the middle or end of the third month of school, we introduce a predictable book along with its pull-through cover. Our goal is to present at least one of these books each quarter of the school year. We usually wait until mid-year to introduce students to flip-books, which require a little more coordination to make and manipulate than pull-throughs and predictable books.

With first-graders, you might introduce flip-books during the first month of the school year either in learning centers or in small groups, then follow up with a new flip-book every few weeks. You can introduce pull-throughs during the first month too, and then present them every two weeks as with kindergartners. When you feel students are ready for the predictable books, probably during the first quarter, you can add them to your program, introducing new books as often as you wish.

★ TEACHING TIP ★

Many students will be excited about reading their phonetic pull-throughs, predictable books, and flip-books to you, their classmates, even the principal and librarian! Others may prefer to have someone read with them or to them, especially if they are unsure of the words. By giving students the option, you'll help reluctant readers feel more comfortable with new words—and at the same time, give other students a chance to share what they know with a varied audience. Because students will probably be eager to bring their pull-throughs, predictable books, and flip-books home, you may want to let them make duplicates—one to read with families and one to use at school.

Rhyming Word Warm-Ups

Prior to introducing the pull-throughs, predictable books, and flip-books, it's helpful to give students some experience with rhyming words. (They might be surprised at how many they already know!) Here are a few warm-up activities to try:

Manipulating Magnetic Letters: Look at rhyming words from favorite stories. Invite children to build those words and others they rhyme with using magnetic or overhead letters. If you don't have enough magnetic letters to go around, you can have children write each letter of the alphabet on a small square of paper and use the letter squares to form rhyming words.

Rhyming Word Stations: Set up rhyming word stations by writing rhyming blends on poster board (one blend per piece), and displaying the poster board around the room with colorful markers, crayons, or pencils. Let children visit the stations and add as many rhyming words as they can to each piece of poster board.

Make a Match: Create pairs of picture cards with rhyming words, such as *cat/bat, star/car, shark/park*. (Include a picture on each card as a visual clue.) Have children play in small groups, taking turns turning over two cards in an effort to make a rhyming match.

Name Game: Encourage children to make strong letter/sound associations using their own names to make rhyming words. (Keep in mind not all names will be easy to rhyme and allow children to form nonsense words).

Rhyming Bingo: Make bingo game boards with rhyming blends across the top and initial consonants below which when combined form words. Be sure to make each board different by varying the consonants that go with the blends. Make a set of initial consonant tiles by writing each on a slip of paper. Place the slips in a bag. When you're ready to play, provide students with chips or other markers, then select a letter from the bag at random and call it out. If students have this letter on their game board, and they can combine it with the rhyming blend at the top

of that column to make a word, they can put a marker over the letter. When students get five markers in a row across, down, or diagonally, have them read the words they formed.

Children's Books

To introduce or reinforce particular rhyming blends, you might want to share some of these engaging books.

ag: *The Bag I'm Taking to Grandma's* by Shirley Neitzel (Greenwillow, 1995)
Our Flag by Carol Memling (Ingram, 1992)

am: *Green Eggs and Ham* by Dr. Seuss (Random House, 1960)
Sam the Scarecrow by Sharon Gordon (Troll, 1980)

an: *Dan, the Flying Man* by Joy Cowley (Thomas C. Wright, 1983)
The Tan Can by Foster and Erickson (Barron's Educational Service, 1992)

ar: *The Story of Babar* by Jean de Brunhoff (Random House, 1966)

ark: *Dinner Time* by Jan Renkowski (Scholastic, 1981)
A Dark, Dark Tale by Ruth Brown (Dial Press, 1981)

at: *The Cat in the Hat* by Dr. Seuss (Random House, 1957)
            Jennie's Hat by Ezra Jack Keats (Trophy, 1985)

ed: *The Big Red Barn* by Margaret Wise Brown (Harper Festival, 1995)
            Time for Bed by Mem Fox (Harcourt Brace, 1993)

eep: *Ba Ba Black Sheep* Mother Goose Rhymes (Silver, Burdett & Ginn, 1989)
            Beep Beep by Barbara Gregorich (School Zone Books, 1992)

ell: *The Snail's Spell* by Joanne Ryder (Viking, 1988)
            Elephant in the Well by Marie Hall (Viking, 1972)

en: *The Little Red Hen* by Lucinda McQueen (Scholastic, 1987)

et: *Emma's Pet* by David McPhail (Penguin, 1988)
            I Want a Pet by Barbara Gregorich (School Zone Books, 1996)

ice: *Chicken Soup With Rice* by Maurice Sendak (Scholastic, 1962)
            If Mice Could Fly by John Cameron (Atheneum, 1979)

ick: *Good Morning, Chick* by Mirrah Ginsburg (Mulberry Books, 1989)

ig: *The Fourth Little Pig* by Teresa Noel Celsi (Raintree/Steck-Vaughn, 1996)
            Pigs Aplenty, Pigs Galore by David McPhail (Puffin, 1997)

in: *In a People House* by Dr. Seuss (Random House, 1989)

ip: *Ship of Dreams* by Dean Morrisey (Harry N. Abrams, 1994)

og: *Clifford the Big Red Dog* by Norman Bridwell (Scholastic, 1985)
Go, Dog, Go by P.D. Eastman (Random House, 1961)

ool: *School* by Emily Arnold McCully (Trophy, 1990)
Timothy Goes to School by Rosemary Wells (E.P. Dutton, 1993)

op: *Hop on Pop* by Dr. Seuss (Random House, 1963)
A Mop For Pop by Kelli C. Foster & Kerri Gifford Russell (Barrons Juveniles, 1991)

ot: *Ten Black Dots* by Donald Crews (Mulberry Books, 1995)
The Empty Pot by Demi (Henry Holt & Co., 1990)

ub: *Rub a Dub Dub* Mother Goose Rhymes (Silver Burdett & Ginn, 1989)
Just Me in the Tub by Mercer Mayer (Western, 1994)

ug: *The Grouchy Ladybug* by Eric Carle (HarperCollins Juvenile, 1996)
A Hundred Hugs by Joy Cowley (Sunshine Books, 1987)

um : *Bubble Gum* by Jan Swartz (Carousel Readers/Dominie Press, 1994)
The Gum Shoe Goose, Private Eye by Mary DeBall Kwitz (Dial Books, 1988)

unch: *The Lunch Box Surprise* by Grace MacCarone (Cartwheel Books, 1995)
Feathers for Lunch by Lois Elhert (Harcourt Brace, 1990)

ut: *Nuts to You* by Lois Elhert (Harcourt Brace, 1993)

Making and Using Phonetic Pull-Throughs

Phonetic pull-throughs provide auditory, visual, and tactile reinforcement of letter identification, letter/sound correspondence, decoding of 3-4 letter phonetic words, and sight word recognition. When children use phonetic pull-throughs, they associate the rhyming blend with a picture, thereby reinforcing the link between meaning and letter/sound correspondence. For example, children associate the *og* rhyming blend with the *dog* character (page 27). When they see other words with the *og* rhyming blend, they are able to decode the words easily because they already have the picture association and sound in their minds.

★ In choosing and using pull-throughs, we've found that it is not necessary that children be able to identify all the letters and sounds contained on a particular pull-through or to be familiar with all the words that are created. In fact, this affords a wonderful opportunity to give students exposure to new letters and sounds, increasing their experience with language and improving their vocabulary.

★ In our experience, it is best to start out making pull-throughs in small groups. Once children understand how to construct a pull-through, you may be able to set up the patterns and supplies at a learning center where children can work independently to make new pull-throughs. In order to keep the activity fresh, you'll want to introduce a new pull-through every couple of weeks.

★ Here's what you'll need to get started, plus directions for assembling the pull-throughs, and ideas for extending the activity. We suggest making a sample to share with students before having them make their own. Talk about the rhyming blend and the many words you can create by pulling the strip through to change the initial consonant. Discuss unfamiliar letters, sounds, or words.

★ TEACHING TIPS ★

★ Try reproducing the phonetic pull-throughs on heavy paper for added durability.

★ You'll notice that double consonants are located at the end of some pull-through strips. If you feel double consonants are too difficult for your students, simply have students snip them off the consonant strip before making the loop.

Materials

★ phonetic pull-through pattern page (one per student)

★ scissors

★ crayons, pens or colored pencils

★ tape

1. Invite students to trace the entire rhyming blend in one color. Have them repeat the rhyming blend sounds as they trace to provide auditory, visual, and tactile reinforcement.

2. Ask your students to trace each of the initial consonants in another color to distinguish them from the rhyming blends. Again, have students repeat each letter sound as they trace it to provide auditory, visual, and tactile reinforcement of letter/sound associations.

3. Have students cut out the phonetic pull-through and initial consonant strip. (Note: Some patterns may be harder for students to cut than others. You can either cut them out beforehand, or leave them

intact and have students simply trim off the consonant strip.) Help them cut the slits on their pull-throughs as indicated by the dashed lines. (Hint: One easy way to cut the slits is to fold the page at a right angle to the dashed lines. Then all you have to do is snip along the lines from the crease of the fold inward.)

4. Have students turn their pull-throughs face-down, thread the strip through the slits and tape the ends of the strip together to form a loop. Then students can turn the pull-through over and pull the loop through to reveal the first initial consonant. If you were using the *ed* pull-through for example (page 19), you would pull the loop so that the letter *b* showed first.

Learning Center Link

In addition to stocking your center with materials for making phonetic pull-throughs, you can set up related activities to reinforce the rhyming word blends. Here are a few suggestions:

★ **Listening for Letter Sounds:** Find stories that contain some of the words featured on a pull-through. (For starters, you might look at the *I Can Read* series by Dr. Seuss, which are very strong in rhyme.) Place the book, a cassette recording of the story (you can record the reading yourself or ask an upper-grade student to help), a tape recorder, and headphones at the center. Invite children to listen to the story as they follow along in the book. Afterwards, have them read through the corresponding pull-through. Ask them what words they recognize from the story.

★ **Make Your Own:** Let students think of new words to go with rhyming blends or vowels you're working on and invite them to create their own phonetic pull-throughs to share. (You might want to provide precut strips of paper for the initial consonants.)

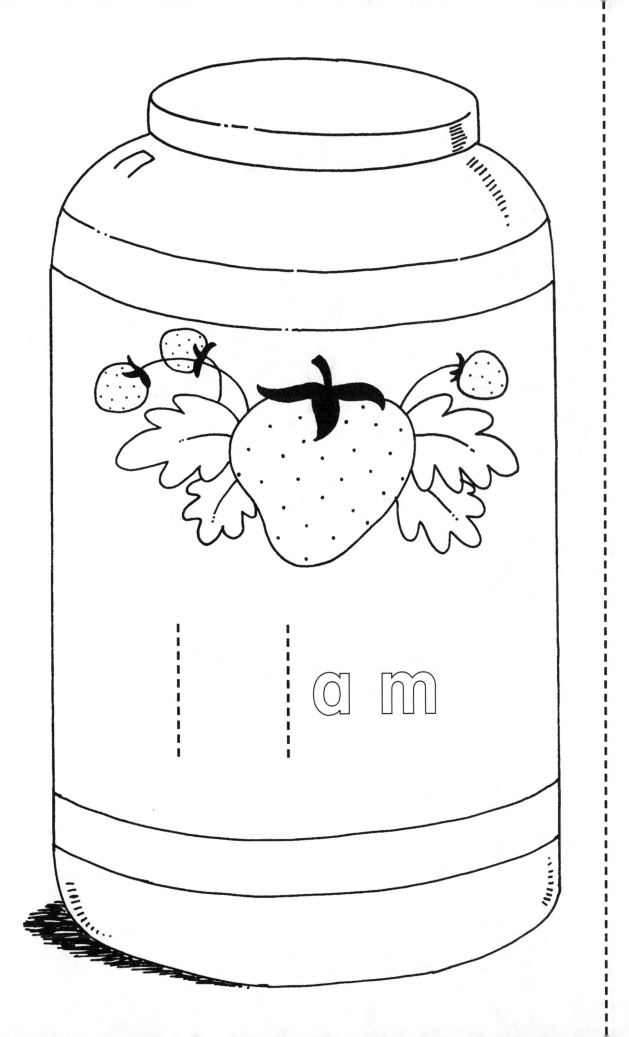

a m

j   r   h   cl

f c m r t v

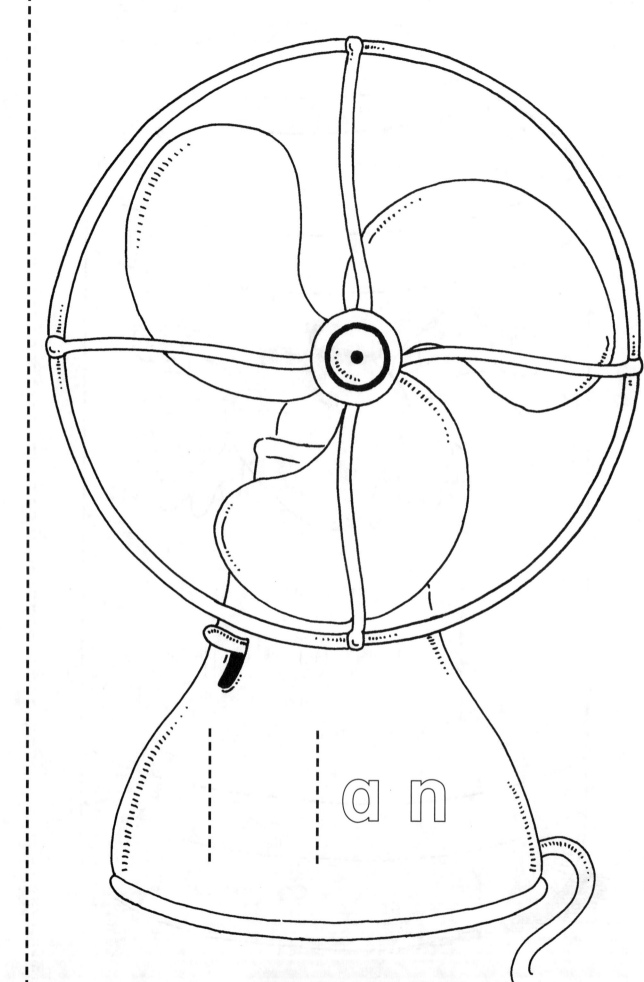

_ _ a n

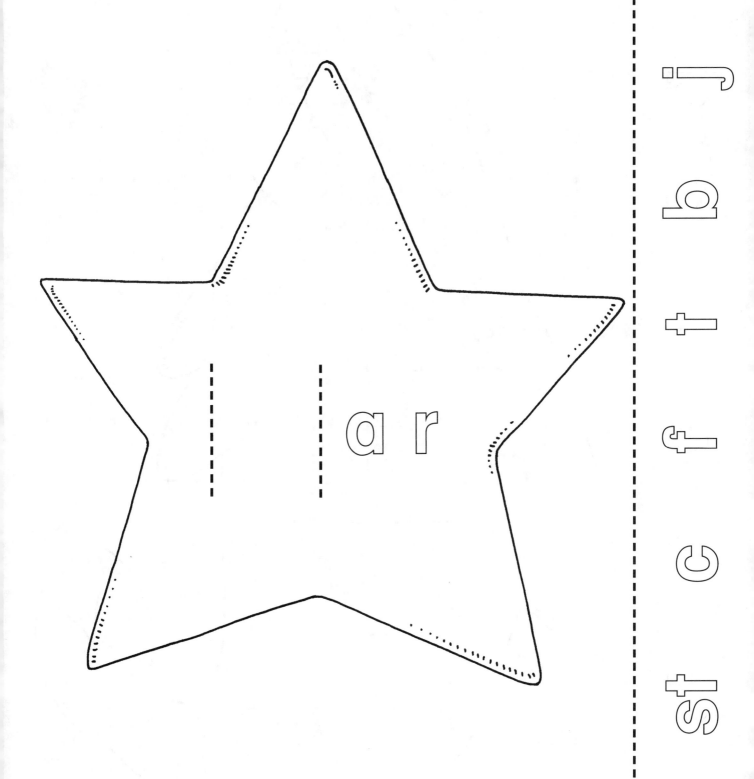

_ _ ar

st c f f t b j

sh b h m p d

_ _ _ _ a r k

_ _ _ _ _ _ _ _

_ _ ed

b f l r w sl

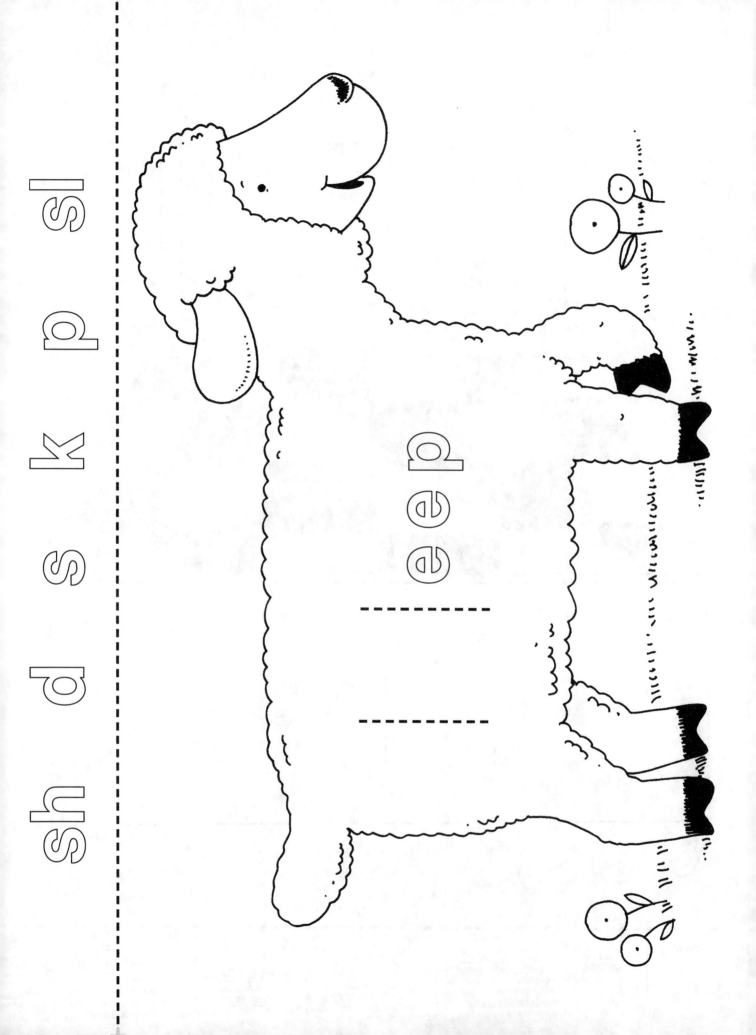

sh d s k p sl

_____ _____ eep

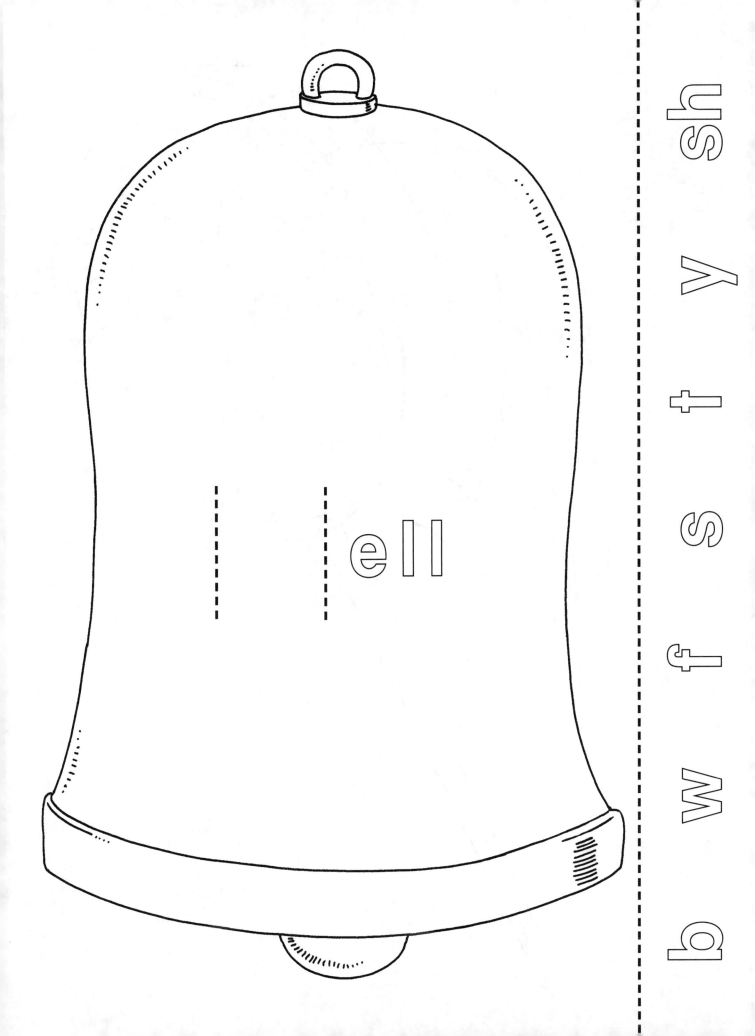

_ _ ell

b w f s t y sh

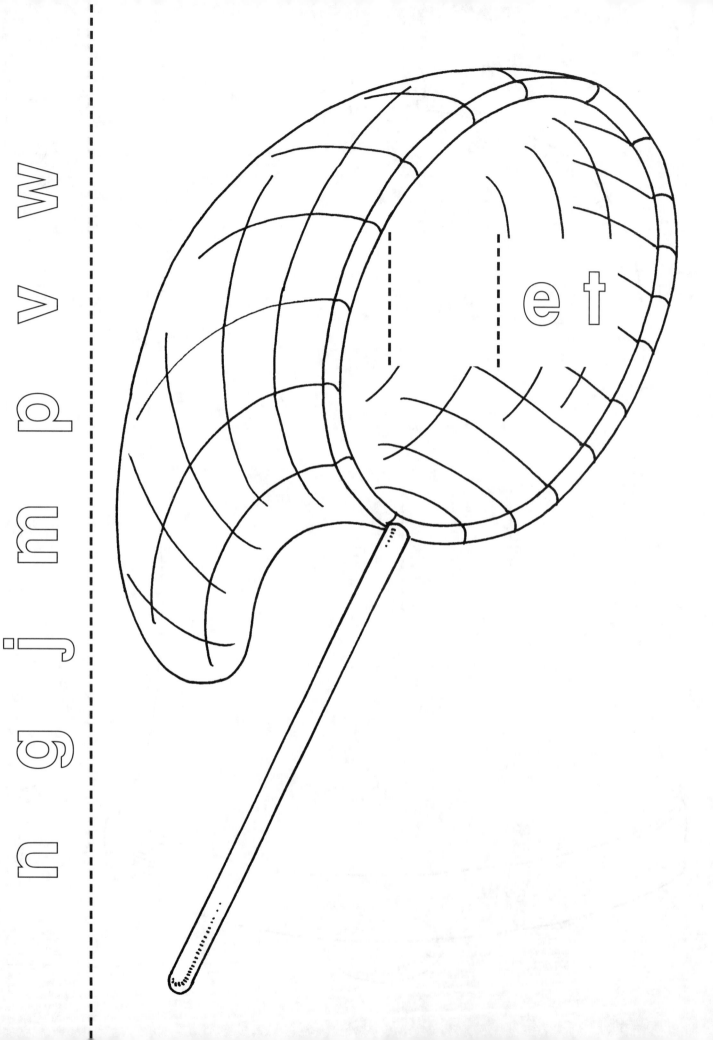

n g j m p v w

u g j m p d v w

e t

_ ice

_ _ _ _ _ _ _ ice

_ _ _ _ _ _ _

m   n   r   d   tw   sp

u

ch   k   l   p   s   br   cl

_ _ _ _ ick

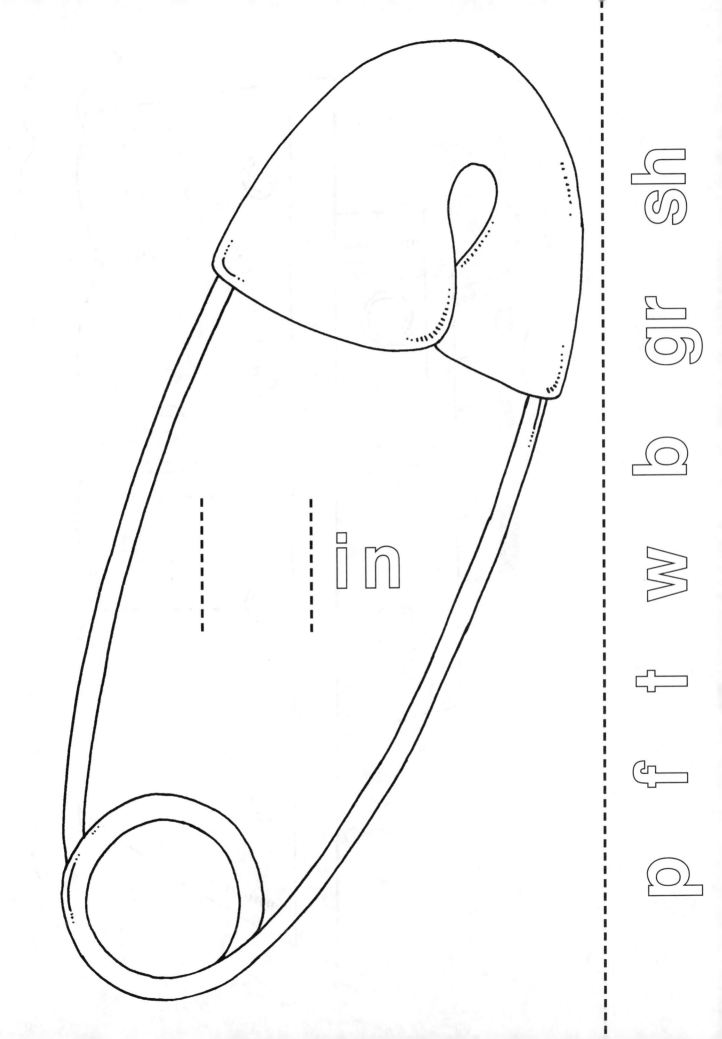

in

p   f   w   b   f   gr   sh

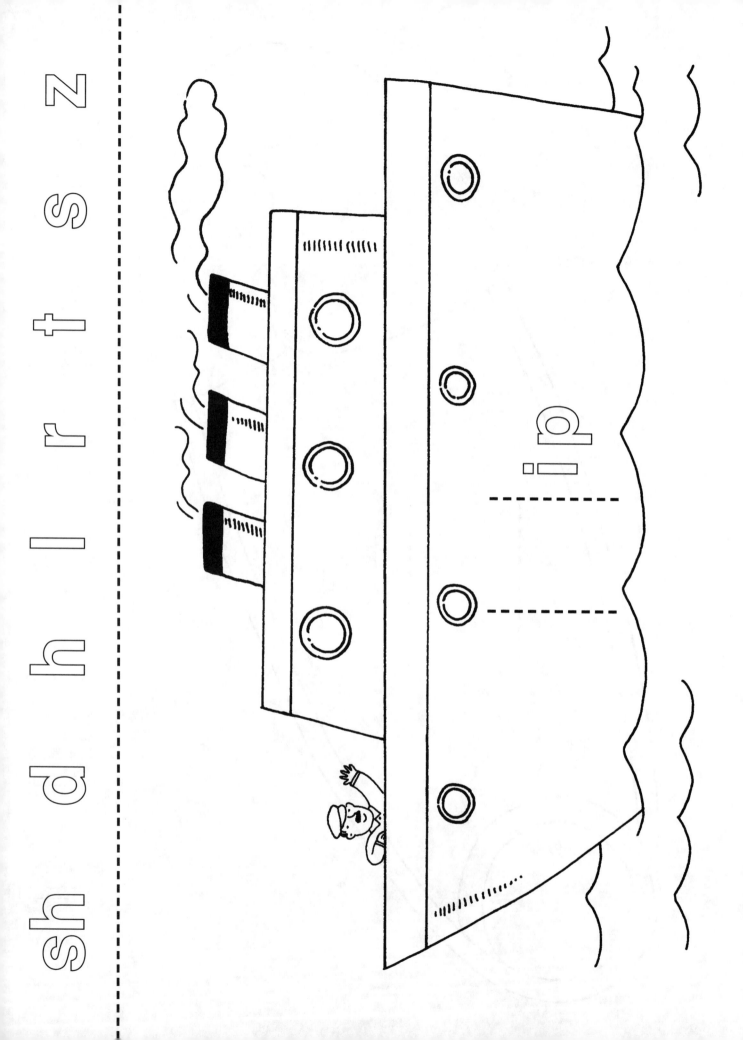

sh   d   h   l   r   t   s   z

_ _ _ _ ip

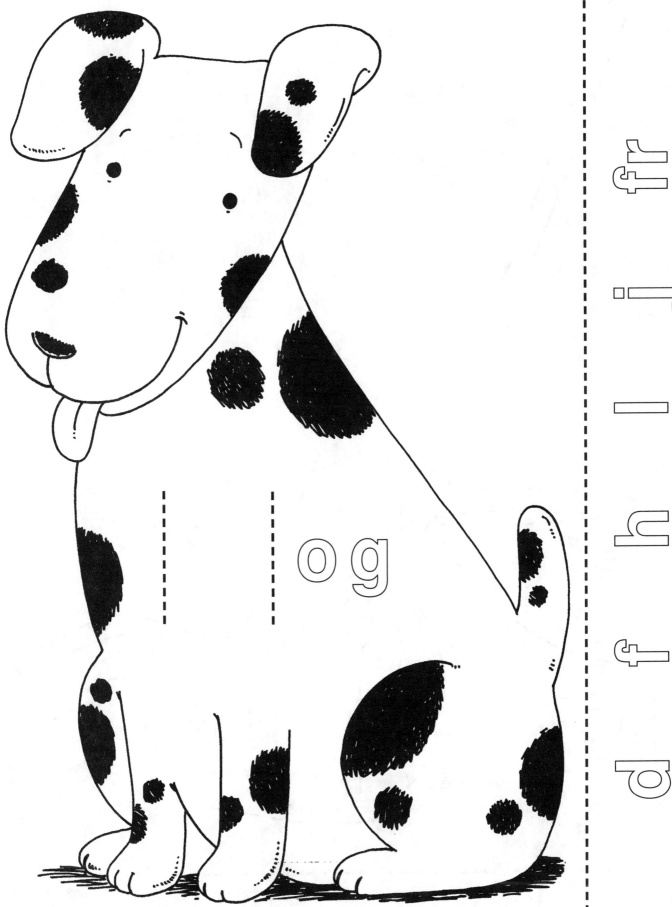

_ _ _ _ _ _ o g

f   d   h   j   l   j   fr

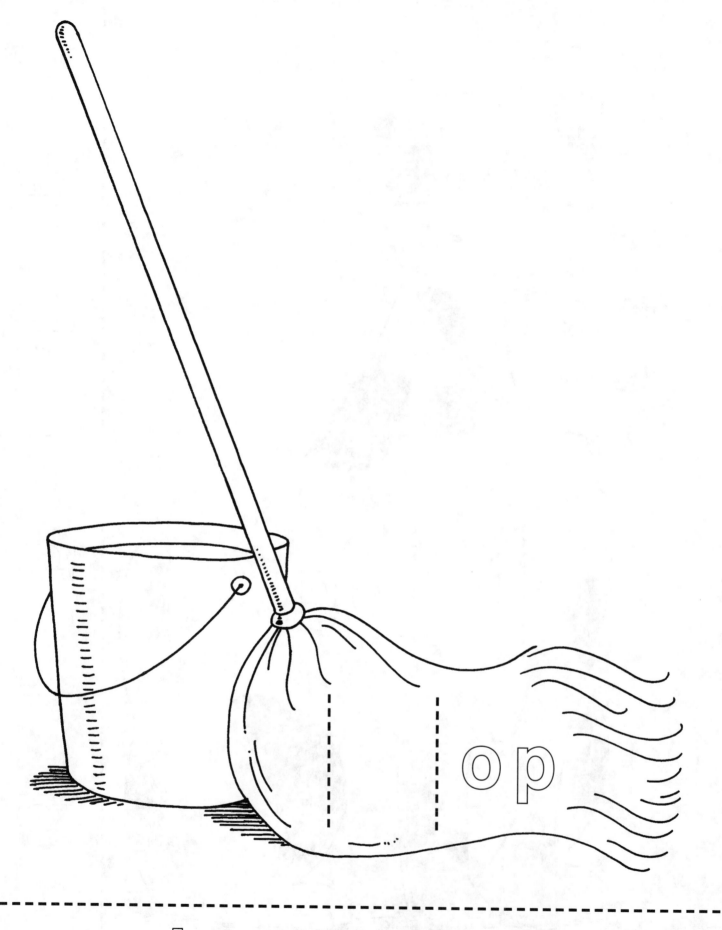

op

m   h   p   t   fl   sh

_ _ ug

b d h j m r t

g h s m ch dr

u m

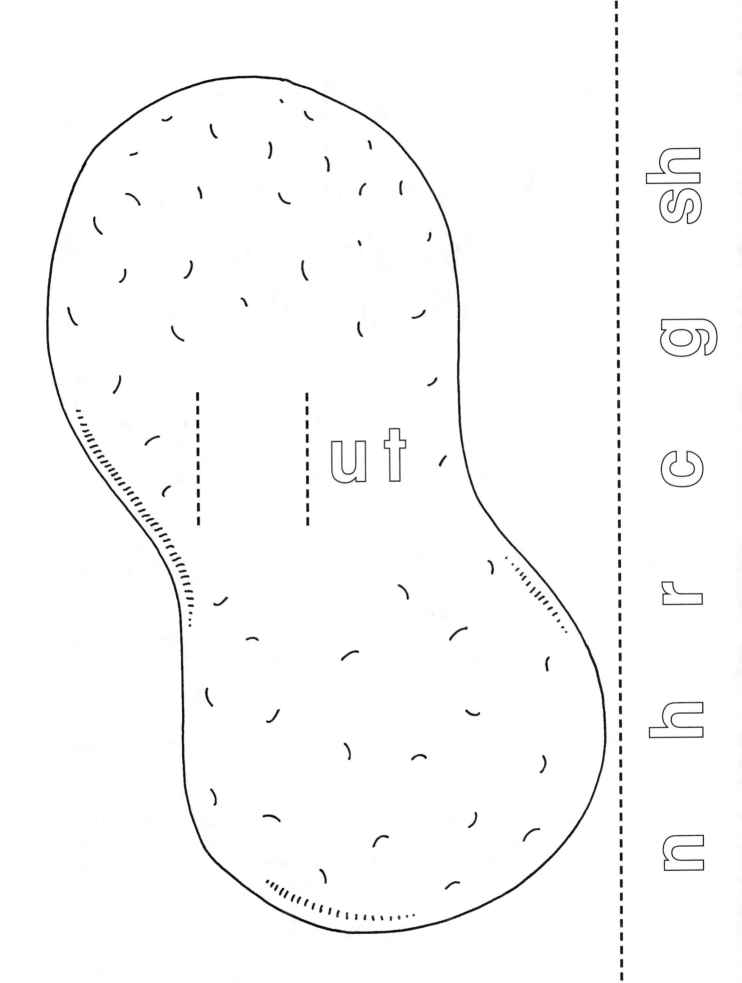

_ _ ut

n h r c g sh

u

Making and Using Pull-Through Predictable Books

Predictable books with pull-through covers are an excellent tool to help your students develop beginning reading skills in a meaningful context. The six pull-through predictable books in this section reinforce letter identification, letter/sound correspondence, and sight word recognition though visual and tactile learning.

Each book pattern in this section features a pull-through cover and one page of incomplete predictable text for students to fill in. Our students love these books because the text is manageable and they get to add their own personal touch. Students can complete as many predictable text pages as they wish, though we've found three to be about right for kindergarten and first grade.

With our kindergarten students, we complete the books over a three day period, scheduling approximately 20 minutes a day for the activity.
- Day 1: We share a sample pull-through predictable book and discuss the rhyming words we can make on the cover and those that appear in the predictable text.
- Day 2: We guide children in making their pull-through covers.
- Day 3: Students put covers and predictable text pages together to make their books.

After completing the pages, we give students time to read their books, both independently and with others.

If you teach first grade, you can probably put the books together over two days. You could share a sample book and make the covers. On Day 2, students could complete the predictable pages and bind their books. Again, give students time to read their books alone, with you, or with other students or teachers.

Materials

* pull-through predictable book pattern pages (cover and text page)

* crayons, pens or colored pencils

* scissors

* tape

1. Make and share a sample pull-through predictable book with as many text pages as you wish. Discuss the rhyming blend and the page shape (e.g. bag, hat), and let students take turns pulling the strip to make new words. Read your book once through. You can either invite students to help you choose words to fill in the blanks, or you can complete the text ahead of time.

2. Give each student a copy of the cover with the pull-through pattern. Invite students to trace the rhyming blend and initial consonants in different colors.

3. Guide students in cutting out the initial consonant strip and cover. Help them cut slits as indicated by the dashed lines.

4. To construct the pull-through cover, have students turn the cover face-down, thread the consonant strip through the slits and tape the ends together to form a loop. Then, ask students to turn the character over and pull the strip through to reveal the first initial consonant (the *B* for

bag; the *P* for *pack* and so on).

5. Have students staple their pull-through covers to multiple predictable text pages. Then, invite them to complete the sentences by filling in the blanks with a word of their choice, and tracing the word the book focuses on (e.g. bag or hat). Some students may prefer to dictate words to you, while others may feel ready to complete the text on their own. In either case, you might want to brainstorm a list of words together for students to choose from.

6. Have students read their predictable books—pull-through covers and all. Take a closer look at students' work by asking questions such as, "What do you notice about the letters and words on the text pages? What other initial consonants could you use to make rhyming words on the cover?" You might even challenge students to take the activity one step further by coming up with rhyming words to complete the text (e.g. A *rag* is in the bag).

sn

bl

s

r

l

b

t

p

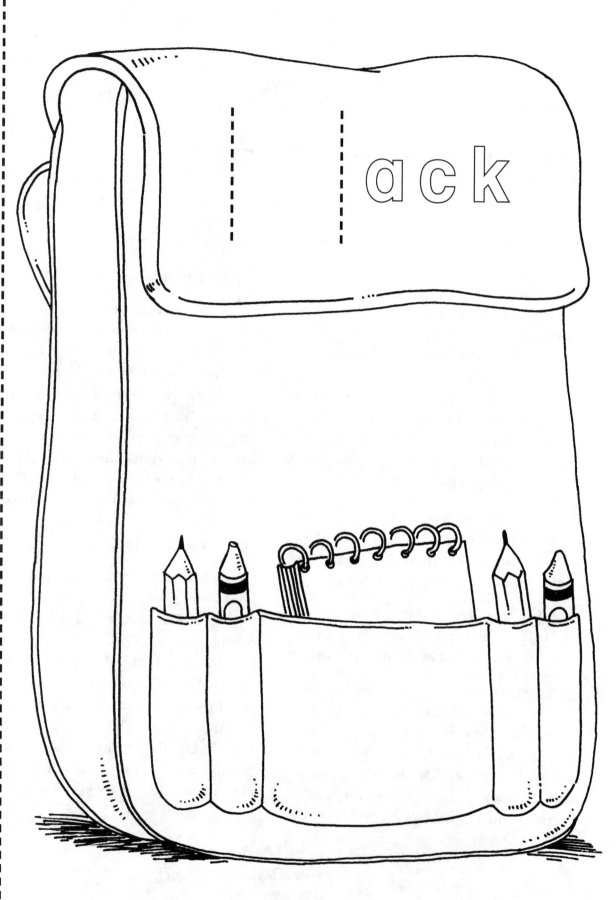

_ _ ack

I put a _____
in my pack.

b r s t w fl

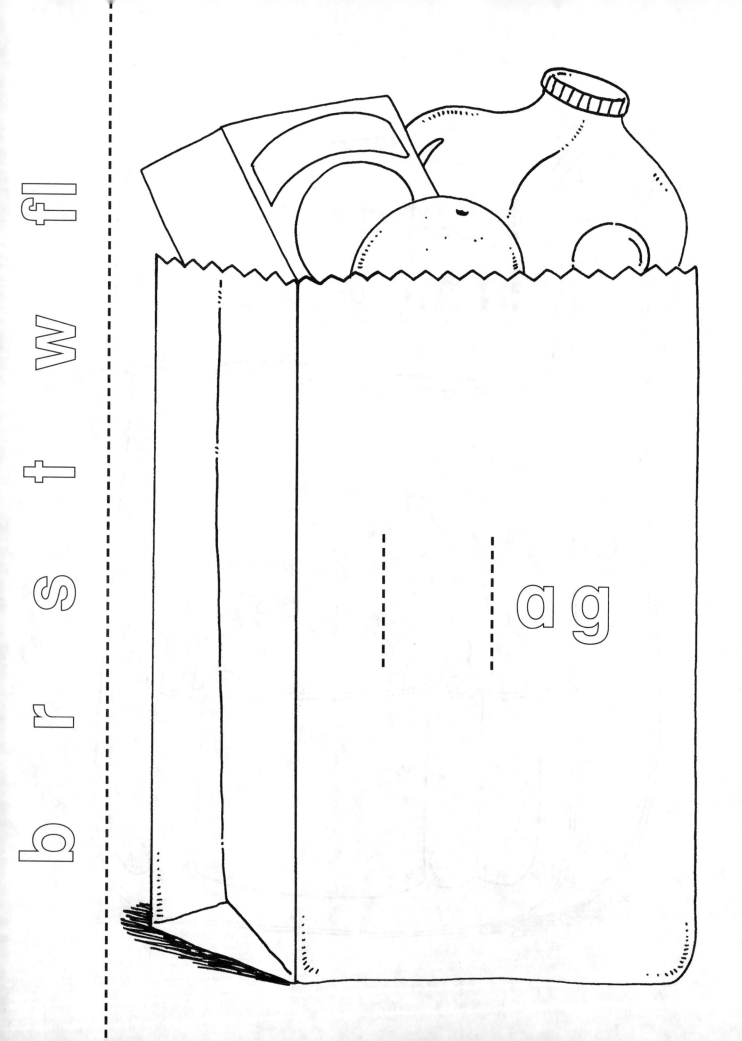

_ _ _ ag

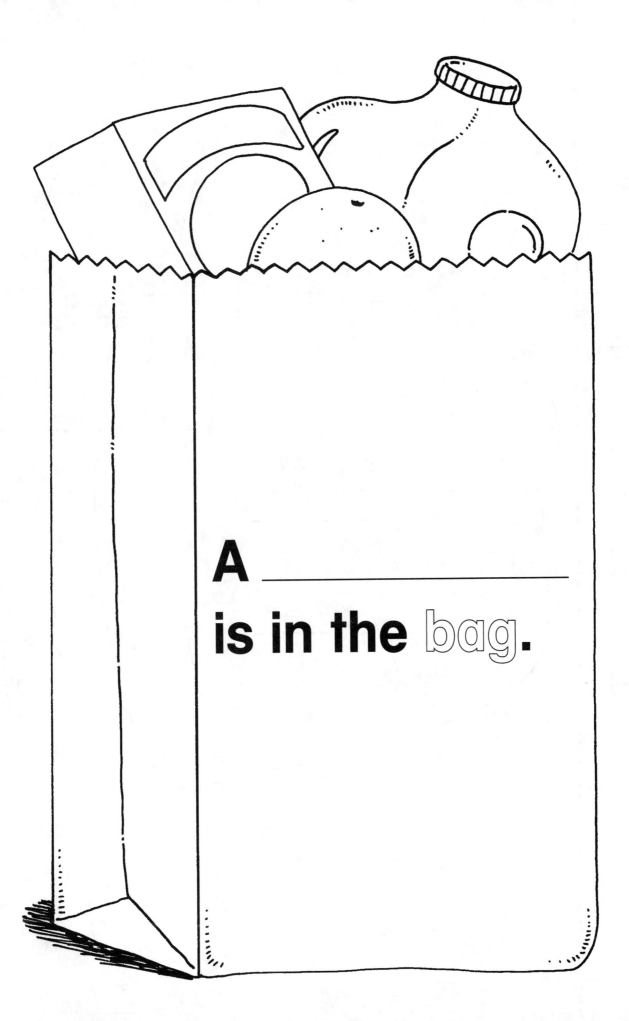

A _____
is in the bag.

h c b m f r s fl

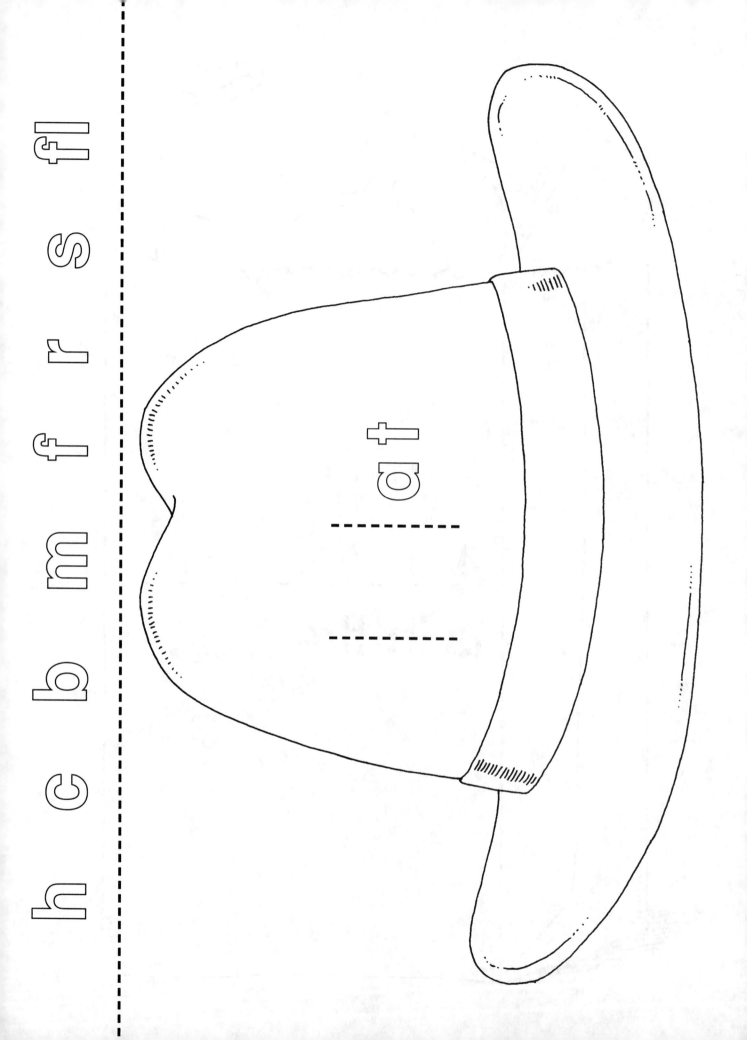

__ __ a t

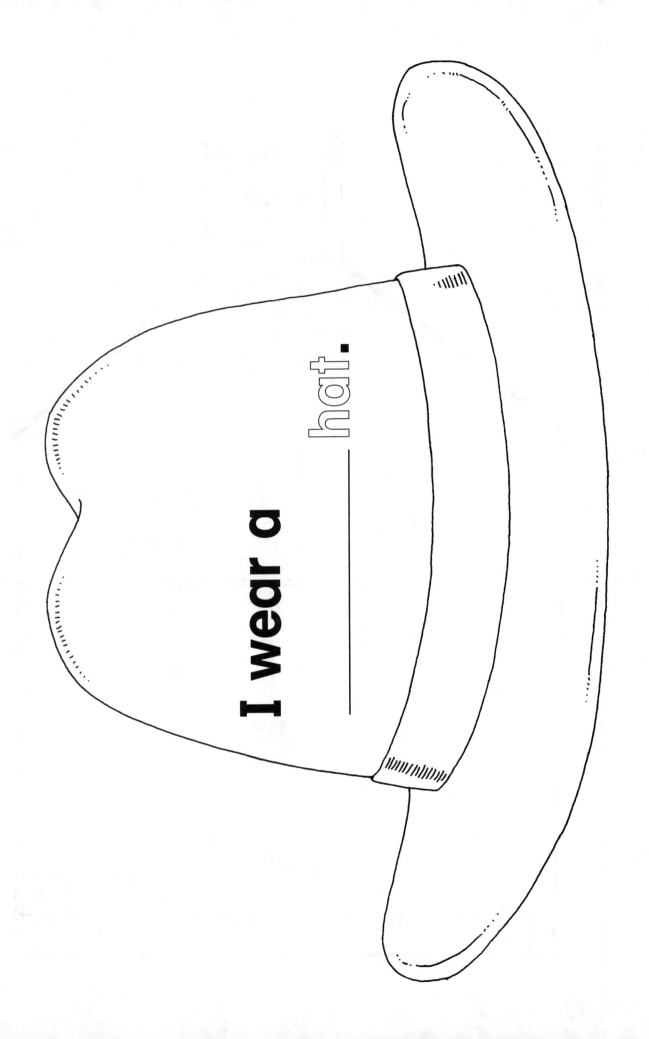

I wear a _____ hat.

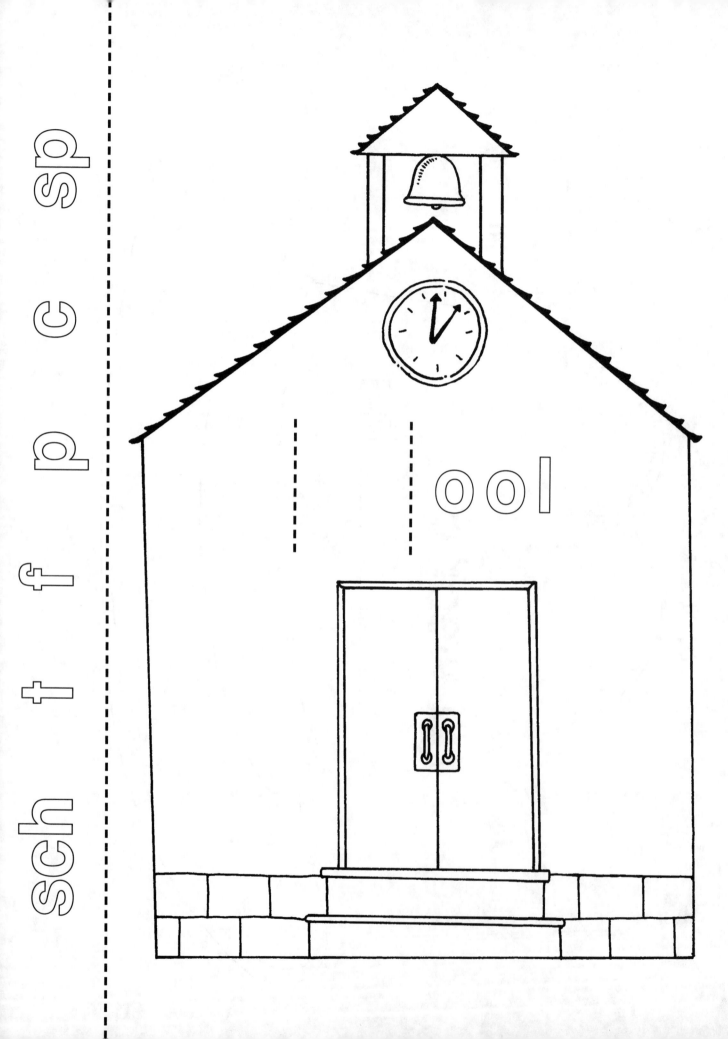

We _____
at school.

_ _ unch

l b m h p cr

I eat _____
for lunch.

Making and Using Rhyming Blend Flip-Books

These self-correcting books provide auditory, visual, and tactile reinforcement of letter identification, letter/sound correspondence, and sight word recognition in a meaningful context. They also help students decode 3-4 letter phonetic words. The illustrations provide a strong visual clue or hook to help students identify the association between letters and sounds and apply what they learn to new words.

Each of the 10 pattern pages here makes one complete flip-book (two flip-books per vowel). Here are the materials you'll need, directions for putting the books together, and suggestions on how to use them.

★ TEACHING TIP ★

Reproduce the flip-book pattern pages on heavy paper, or laminate if possible, for added durability. Make and display a sample flip-book so that students can visualize the steps they'll have to take to assemble their own book.

Materials

★ flip-book pattern page (one per student)

★ crayons, pens or colored pencils

★ scissors

★ hole punch

★ 4-by-6-inch index cards (one per student)

★ glue

★ brass fasteners (two per student)

1. Ask students to trace the entire rhyming blend in one color, repeating the sounds at the same time to provide auditory, visual, and tactile reinforcement of the letters and their sounds.

2. Have students trace each of the initial consonants in another color to distinguish them from the rhyming blend. Again, let students repeat each sound as they trace the corresponding letter.

3. Have students cut along the solid lines to create one rhyming blend page and multiple initial consonant and picture pages. As students cut the pages apart, have them draw a circle or dot on the back of each, using a different color for each pair of initial consonant and picture pages. For example, students would place matching marks on the back of the *m* page and the *mop* illustration of the *op* book. As students form and read new words, they can look to these dots to check their work themselves.

4. Ask students to glue their rhyming blend pages to the index cards and punch holes at the top of the pages, using the circles as guides.

5. Help students attach the initial consonant and picture pages to the rhyming blend page using brass fasteners. A couple of options for page arrangement follow.

• Fasten the initial consonant and the corresponding picture pages side-by-side.

• Mix the picture and consonant cards for an added challenge. (In this case, students find the illustration that corresponds to the initial consonant before forming the rhyming word.)

In either case, students can check their work by looking on the back of the picture and consonant cards to see if the colored dots match.

Learning Center Link

Rather than put the flip-books together as a class, your students may be able to work independently at a learning center to make their books. In this case, just stock your center with the necessary materials (see page 44), and display a sample book for students to use as a guide.

If you make the books as a class, you can use your learning center to offer follow-up activities like these:

★ **Create Your Own Flip-Books:** Provide blank flip-book templates so that students can create their own rhyming blend, initial consonant, and picture pages. Whether students make books using familiar words and illustrations or invent their own, these personalized flip-books are a hit.

★ **Play with Poems:** Display poetry that uses some of the same rhyming words as the flip-book students are making. Copy the poems on chart paper, leaving blanks for the rhyming words. Write those words on cards and glue Velcro™ to the back side of the cards and the blanks on the chart. Invite students to complete the poem, placing the words where they go.

can
fan
man
pan
van

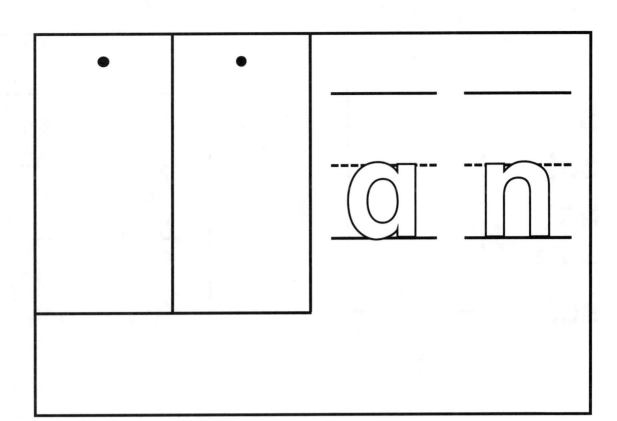

bat
cat
hat
mat
sat

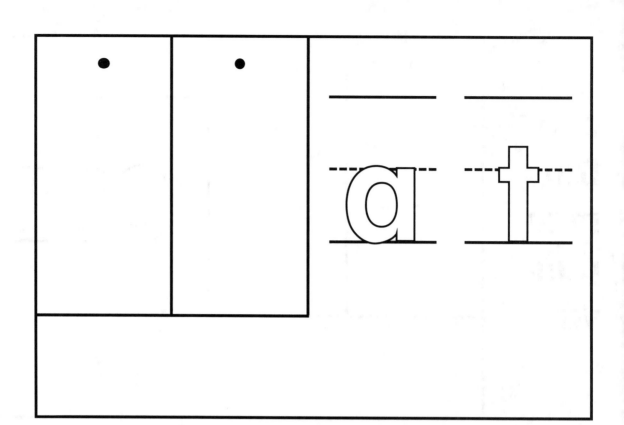

_ a t

b c h m s

hen

men

pen

ten

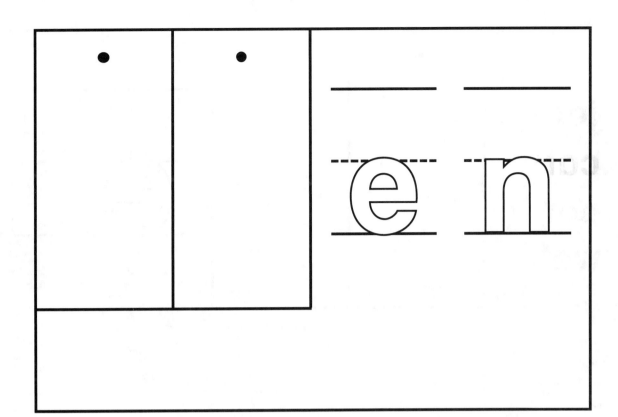

jet
net
pet
wet

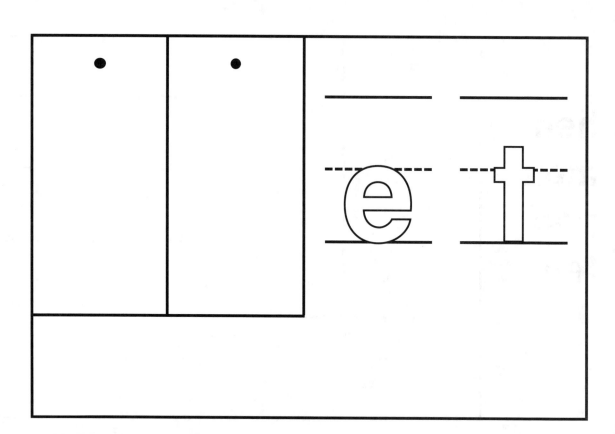

dig
jig
pig
wig

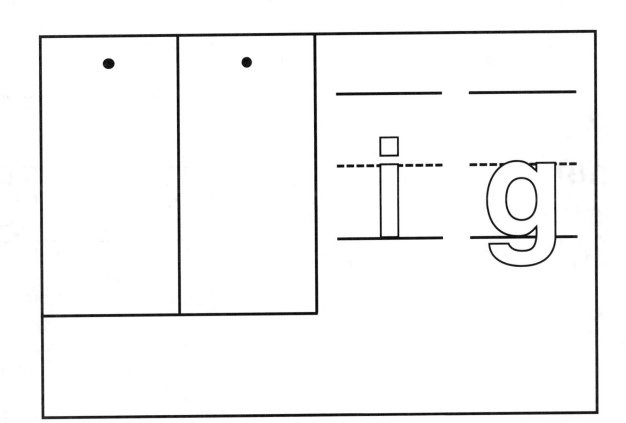

i g

d   j   p   w

zip
rip
ship
hip

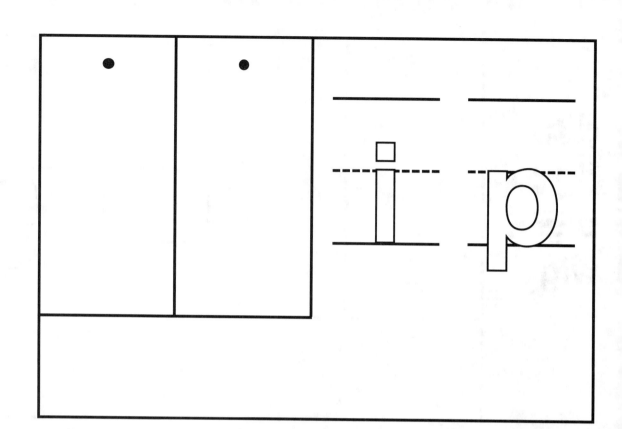

hop

mop

pop

top

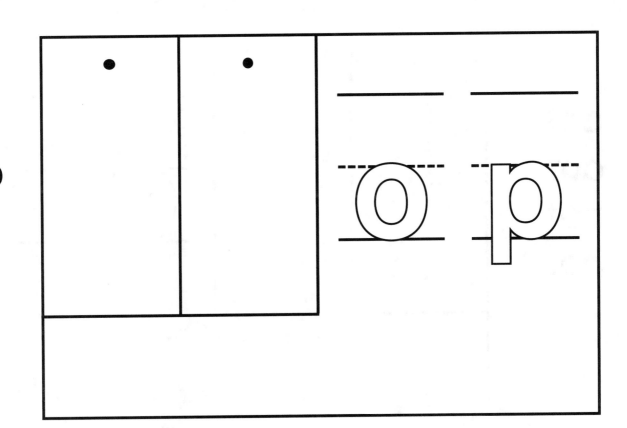

dot
cot
hot
pot

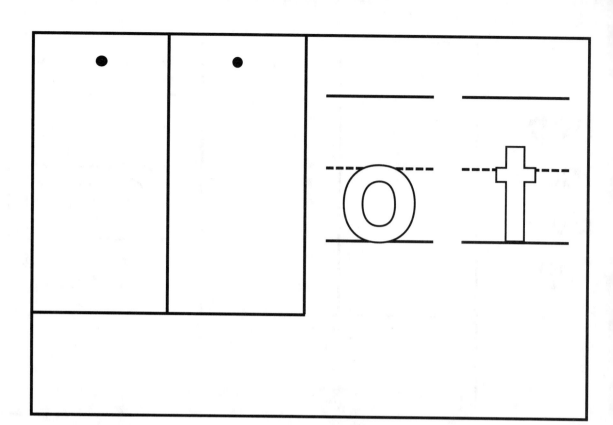

sub

cub

rub

tub

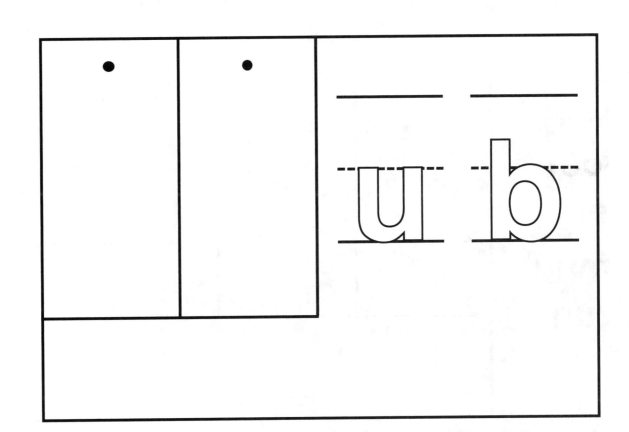

bug
hug
jug
mug
rug